JESUS OUR GUIDE
Activity Book

JESUS OUR GUIDE

Activity Book

Faith and Life Series

BOOK FOUR

Ignatius Press, San Francisco
Catholics United for the Faith, New Rochelle

Nihil Obstat: Daniel V. Flynn, J.C.D.
                 Censor Librorum
Imprimatur: + Joseph T. O'Keefe, D.D.
                 Vicar General, New York

Director: Rev. Msgr. Eugene Kevane, Ph.D.
Assistant Director and General Editor: Patricia I. Puccetti, M.A.
Writer: Barbara Nacelewicz
Map: Gregory P. Hartnell
Artist: Gary Hoff

Catholics United for the Faith, Inc., and Ignatius Press gratefully acknowledge the guid-
ance and assistance of Reverend Monsignor Eugene Kevane, former Director of the
Pontifical Catechetical Institute, Diocese of Arlington, Virginia, in the production of this
series. The series intends to implement the authentic approach in Catholic catechesis given
to the Church in the recent documents of the Holy See and in particular the Conference of
Joseph Cardinal Ratzinger on "Sources and Transmission of Faith".

Contents

1. The Fall of Man 7
2. The World's First Murder 8
3. Turning away from God 10
4. God Prepares a People for the Savior 11
5. The People of Israel 13
6. Joseph Goes to Egypt 14
7. The People of Israel Go to Egypt 16
8. God's People Suffer in Egypt 19
9. God Saves His People 21
10. Great Things Happen on the Way to the Promised Land 23
11. Life in the Promised Land 25
12. A King for God's People 27
13. King David 28
14. King Solomon and the Promise of a New King 29
15. The Final King 31
16. An Invitation to Heaven 33
17. Road Signs along the Way 35
18. Loving Others 36
19. Growing in Love 38
20. Jesus, Our Guide 41
21. "For This I Have Come into the World" 42
22. The Perfect Sacrifice 44
23. Bread from Heaven 45
24. Mistakes along the Way 47
25. Turning back to God 48
26. The Holy Spirit 50
27. The Church of Christ 52
28. Channels of Grace 54
29. Our Mother, Mary 57
30. We Reach our Goal 59
    Advent and Christmas Supplement 60
    Lent and Easter Supplement 61
    Appendix 62

CHAPTER 1

The Fall of Man

I. Use your book to answer the following questions:

1. What was the name of the tree which God told Adam and Eve not even to touch?

   _____

2. Who disguised himself as a serpent in order to get Eve to disobey God? _____

   _____

3. After Adam and Eve had disobeyed God, what did they do when they heard him

   walking in the garden? _____

   _____

   _____

4. Whom did Adam blame for his sin? _____

5. Whom did Eve blame for her sin? _____

6. What was Adam and Eve's punishment? _____

   _____

II. On the lines below, write as many words as you can think of describing Adam and
Eve *before* and *after* they disobeyed God.

before the Fall:	**after the Fall:**
_____	_____
_____	_____
_____	_____
_____	_____
_____	_____

CHAPTER 2

The World's First Murder

I. Use your book to answer these questions:

1. What did Abel do for a living? _____

2. What did Cain do for a living? _____

3. What did both Cain and Abel do to honor God? _____

_____

_____

4. Whose sacrifice was God pleased with? _____

5. Why? _____

_____

_____

6. Who warned Cain that he must overcome his anger? _____

7. What did Cain do to Abel? _____

_____

8. What was Cain's punishment? _____

_____

_____

9. What did God do to make sure that no one would harm Cain? _____

_____

10. What was the name of Adam and Eve's third son, who was born after Abel was

killed? _____

II. Unscramble the words below to find the question that Cain asked God when God asked him where Abel was.

"MA I YM TROSHERB' PEKERE?"

"_____ __ ____ _____ _____?"

If God had answered Cain's question, what do you think he would have said? _____

_____

_____

_____

CHAPTER 3

Turning away from God

I. Fill in the blanks in questions 1–5 to complete the word train just below. *Hint*: The last letter of each word is the first letter in the word that follows it. Use your book if you need help.

1 r a i n B o 2 v o t e 3 r a i 4 n o a d 5 h a m

1. God put a __rainbow__ in the sky as a sign of his promise never again to send a great flood to destroy the earth.
2. When the dove came back with an olive branch in her beak, Noah knew that the __water__ was nearly gone from the earth.
3. God made it __rain__ for forty days and forty nights.
4. God told __Noah__ to build an ark.
5. Noah's son, __Ham__, had a son named Canaan.

II. Use your book to fill in the blanks below. Then copy the letters in the boxes onto the tower to see what the sin of the people who built the Tower of Babel was.

Some 1. [P] e o p l e migrated to the land of Shinar.

They thought that they could build a 2. t o w e [r] with its top in the heavens.

Higher and 3. H [i] g h e r up went the tower.

But God was not pleased with their 4. P r o u [d] hearts.

He confused their 5. l a n g u a g [e], making them unable to complete their tower.

1. P
2. r
3. i
4. d
5. e

CHAPTER 4

God Prepares a People
For the Savior

I. Use your book to solve this crossword puzzle:

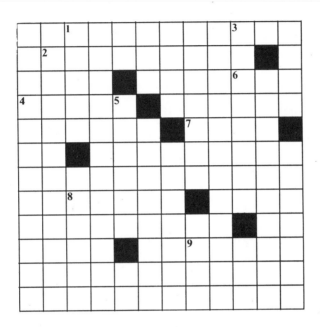

Across

2. What God told Abraham to do with Isaac.
4. Abraham and Sarah's only son.
6. The name of Abraham's nephew.
7. Abraham was a descendant of _____.
8. God told Abraham his descendants would be as many as the _____ in the sky.
9. Abraham's name before God changed it.

Down

1. The wife of Abraham.
3. Abraham always _____ God.
5. The name of the land that God promised to the descendants of Abraham.
8. The name of the city Abraham saved.

II. Reread the account in your book of how God made the covenant with Abraham. Then see if you can fill in the blanks in the Bible account below, using the following words: Canaan, God, fell, Almighty, covenant, Abraham, Abram, blameless.

"When Abram was ninety-nine years old the Lord appeared to Abram, and said to him, 'I am God _____; walk before me, and be _____. And I will make my _____ between me and you. . . .' Then Abram _____ on his face; and God said to him, '. . . No longer shall your name be _____ but your name shall be _____; for I have made you the father of a multitude of nations. . . . And I will give to you and to your descendants after you . . . all the land of _____ for an everlasting possession; and I will be their _____.' "

(Genesis 17:1—8)

CHAPTER 5

The People of Israel

Write "T" if a statement is true; write "F" if it is false. *Hint*: Use your book to help you, and read these sentences *very* carefully!

F 1. Isaac's wife's name was Rachel.

T 2. Isaac and Rebekah had two sons, whom they named Jacob and Esau.

F 3. Jacob loved to hunt.

T 4. Jacob sold his birthright to Esau for a bowl of stew.

T 5. Rebekah helped Jacob to get Isaac's blessing instead of Esau.

T 6. When Esau discovered that Jacob had received Isaac's blessing, he wanted to kill Jacob.

T 7. While Jacob was hiding from Esau in Haran, he married a woman named Leah.

T 8. While Jacob was hiding from Esau in Haran, he married a woman named Rachel.

F 9. While Jacob was hiding from Esau in Haran, he married a woman named Rebekah.

T 10. One of Jacob and Leah's children was named Judah.

T 11. Jesus is a descendant of Judah.

T 12. Jacob and Rachel's two sons were Benjamin and Joseph.

F 13. Isaac's new name was Israel.

T 14. Jacob is the same person as Israel.

F 15. Jacob's descendants were known as the people of Jacob.

CHAPTER 6

Joseph Goes to Egypt

I. Can you fill in the missing words? Use your book if you need help.

Israel ♡ + d _Loved_ all his ☀ + s _sons_ but he

especially ♡ + d _Loved_ Joseph. He made him a 🧥 _coat_

out of fine cloth. When the brothers 🪚 _saw_ this, they were full of **N + V**

envy. Then Joseph had a dream that his brothers' bundles of 🌾

hay bowed ⬇ _down_ to his own. His brothers **h + 8 + ed**

hated him and wanted to kill him. They ⚓ + **ld** _sold_ him to some

🧺 + **ders** _traders_ going to Egypt. But Joseph became a favorite of

fair + 🚣 _fairow_ by telling him about the seven **y** + 👂 + **s**

years of famine that were going to come upon Egypt.

II. Reread the account in your book of how Joseph was sold by his brothers into slavery. Then see if you can fill in the blanks in the Bible account below, using the following words: camels, dreamer, eat, Joseph, twenty, blood, kill, Egypt, beast, sell, bring, goat, brother, throw.

''Now [Joseph's] brothers went to pasture their father's flocks near Shechem. And Israel said to Joseph . . . , 'Go now, see if it is well with your brothers and _____ me word again'. . . . So Joseph went after his brothers, and found them at Dothan. They saw him afar off, and . . . said to one another, 'Here comes this _____. Come now, let us _____ him and _____ him into one of the pits; then we shall say that a wild _____ has devoured him. . . .'' And Reuben said to them, 'Shed no _____; cast him into this pit here in the wilderness' . . . that he might . . . restore him to his father. So when _____ came to his brothers, they stripped him of his robe . . . and cast him into a pit. . . . Then they sat down to _____; and looking up they saw a caravan of Ishmaelites . . . with their _____ bearing gum, balm, and myrrh on their way to carry it down to _____. Then Judah said to his brothers, 'Come let us _____ him to the Ishmaelites, and let not our hand be upon him, for he is our _____'. . . . and they drew Joseph out of the pit and sold him to the Ishmaelites for _____ shekels of silver; and they took Joseph to Egypt. . . . Then they took Joseph's robe, and killed a _____, and dipped the robe in the blood . . . and brought it to their father.''

(Genesis 37:2−32)

15

CHAPTER 7

The People of Israel
Go to Egypt

I. Put an **X** in front of the group of words that completes each sentence below. Use your book if you need help.

1. Israel sent ten of his sons to Egypt

    _____ to see the sights.

    _____ to buy a house there.

    __X__ to buy food.

2. When Joseph saw his brothers he

    __X__ pretended not to know them.

    _____ threw them all in prison.

    _____ threw a party for them.

3. Joseph cried because he could see

    _____ that his brothers were hungry.

    __X__ that his brothers were sorry for having sold him.

    _____ that his brothers were *not* sorry for having sold him.

4. Joseph sent his brothers home the first time so that

    __X__ they could return with Benjamin.

    _____ they could say hello to their father.

    _____ they could have a vacation.

5. Finally, with Benjamin in Egypt, Joseph

    _____ had all his brothers thrown in prison.

    __X__ told his brothers who he really was.

    _____ told his brothers to go home and never bother him again.

6. Joseph told his brothers not to be upset about selling him as a slave because

    _____ Joseph had enjoyed every minute of being a slave.

    _____ he was still going to get even with them for it.

    __X__ God had allowed it to happen so that he could save his chosen people from starvation.

7. When Joseph sent for his father, Israel, to join him in Egypt, Israel

    _____ left for Egypt immediately

    __X__ was not sure if he should leave the promised land of Canaan to go to Egypt.

    _____ did not ever want to see Joseph again.

8. When Israel died in Egypt, Joseph

    _____ buried him in Egypt.

    _____ left Egypt and never came back.

    __X__ took his body back to Canaan and buried him beside Abraham, Isaac, Rebekah, and Leah.

II. Three of Joseph's brothers are mentioned in Chapter 7 of the text. Can you name them?

    1. _Benjamin_____

    2. _Judah_____

    3. _Reuben_____

III. Can you answer these questions? Use the book if you need help.

1. Which brother wanted to sell Joseph to the traders? _____

2. What good thing did that brother do when Joseph said he was going to take Benjamin
   for his slave? _____

   _____

   _____

3. What do you think that tells us about his brother? _____

   _____

   _____

   _____

CHAPTER 8

God's People Suffer in Egypt

I. Use your book to help you find the answers hidden in the pyramid. *Hint*: The words can be spelled in any direction.

```
                        P
                    H   S   R
                A   E   G   M   I
            R   S   B   O   R   N   N
        A   O   R   R   D   O   A   D   C
    O   M   D   L   E   V   I   A   M   E   E
H   S   Y   A   H   W   E   H   W   B   H   G   S
S   L   A   V   E   S   S   I   V   C   E   K   A   N   S
```

1. Pharaoh decided to make the Hebrews _____.

2. Who decided to put all the boy babies of the Hebrews to death?

3. Who were the people who suffered in Egypt?

4. One day a little boy was _____ into the tribe of _____.

5. The little boy's name was _____.

6. The daughter of Pharaoh was a _____.

7. Who talked to Moses from the burning bush?

8. What did God tell Moses his name is?

9. What is the Hebrew word meaning ''I Am''?

II. In the space below, draw one of the following:

1. The baby Moses in the basket being rescued by Pharaoh's daughter.

2. God talking to Moses from the burning bush.

CHAPTER 9

God Saves His People

I. Fill in the missing words. You may use your book.

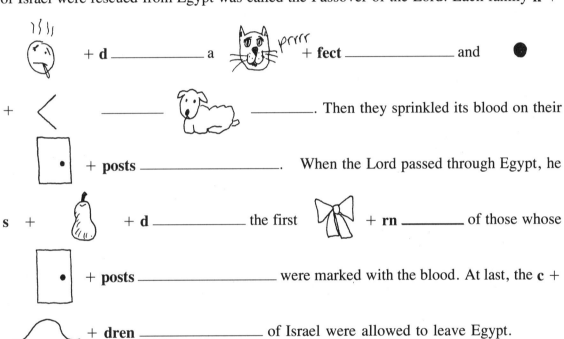

The **n** + 👁 + **t** _____ the **c** + ⌒ + **dren** _____

of Israel were rescued from Egypt was called the Passover of the Lord. Each family **k** +

😷 + **d** _____ a 🐱 prrrr + **fect** _____ and ●

+ < _____ 🐑 _____ . Then they sprinkled its blood on their

▯ + **posts** _____. When the Lord passed through Egypt, he

s + 🍐 + **d** _____ the first 🎀 + **rn** _____ of those whose

▯ + **posts** _____ were marked with the blood. At last, the **c** +

⌒ + **dren** _____ of Israel were allowed to leave Egypt.

II. Use your book to list the ten plagues that came upon Egypt:

1. _____

2. _____

3. _____

4. _____

5. _____

6. _____

7. _____

8. _____

9. _____

10. _____

III. Why is the special meal that the Jews eat every year called Passover? Look in your book to find the answer. _____

_____

_____

CHAPTER 10

Great Things Happen on the Way To the Promised Land

I. Unscramble the words in parentheses to complete the sentences below. Use your book if you need help.

1. When the people of Israel ran out of (odfo) _food_, God sent a heavy dew to cover the ground.

2. When the dew evaporated, it left behind white, flaky (drabe) _bread_, which tasted of honey.

3. They called it (nmnaa) _manna_.

4. God provided fresh manna each (groimnn) _morning_ for the rest of the time that the Hebrews were in the desert.

II. Number the sentences in the order in which the events they describe happened.

_5_ The people had a feast to honor the golden calf.

_1_ Moses went up Mount Sinai to spend forty days and forty nights speaking with the Lord.

_3_ Moses came down from the mountain, threw down the tablets with the Commandments, and punished the people for their sin.

_2_ God gave Moses the Ten Commandments carved on stone tablets.

_4_ The people of Israel grew tired of waiting for Moses, and so they gave their gold jewelry to Aaron who made a golden calf out of it.

III. Read the description of the Ark of the Covenant in your book. Then, in the space below, draw a picture of what you think it must have looked like.

CHAPTER 11

Life in the Promised Land

I. Fill in the crossword puzzle with the correct words.

"Big J" Crossword

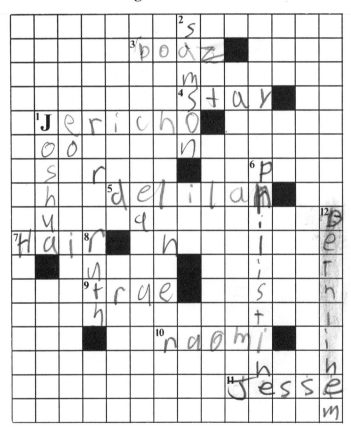

Across
 1. What was the first city Joshua conquered?
 3. Naomi's relative from Bethlehem who married Ruth.
 4. Ruth said that wherever Naomi stayed, she would _____.
 5. Who begged and coaxed Samson to tell her his secret?
 7. Samson was strong as long as he did not cut his _____.
 9. Ruth came to call the one, _____ God her own.
10. The name of Ruth's mother-in-law.
11. Ruth and Boaz had a son named Obed who became the father of _____.

  1. God appointed a man named _____ to take Moses' place as leader.

  2. Whom did God send to rescue the people of Israel from the Philistines?

  6. The powerful and warlike people who were always attacking the Hebrews.

  8. Who left her own country and gods to worship the one, true God?

12. After the famine was over, Ruth went with Naomi to live in _____.

Diagonal

  1. The people of Israel crossed the _____ river into the promised land.

CHAPTER 12

A King for God's People

I. Fill in the crossword puzzle with the correct words.

A Royal Crossword

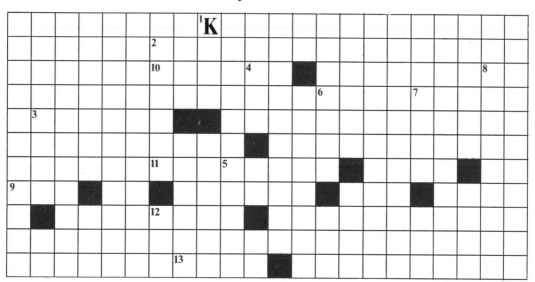

Across
3. The name of the prophet through whom God spoke to his people at the time of King Saul.
9. The name of the priest who was in charge of the tabernacle when Samuel was taken by his mother to Shiloh.
10. The name of Samuel's mother.
11. Saul was very tall and _____.
12. When the people saw Saul standing head and shoulders above them, they cried, "Long live the _____."
13. God said that by asking for a human king, they were rejecting him as _____.
14. Samuel told Saul that God cares more about _____ than sacrifices.

Down
1. The people of Israel wanted to have a _____ like other nations.
2. The place where Eli, the priest in charge of the ark, lived; also the place where the ark was kept.
3. The first king of Israel.
4. What the Hebrews carried into battle and what the Philistines captured.
5. The name of the Philistine's God.
6. As Samuel walked away from Saul, Saul grabbed his _____ and tore it.
7. Because Saul disobeyed God, God rejected him as _____.
8. Samuel told Saul that God was going to make a better man than him _____.

CHAPTER 13

King David

I. Here is the story from the Bible of how David danced before the ark. See if you can fill in the blanks using the following words: danced, harps, ark, merry, Lord, sound, might.

"And David and all the house of Israel were making _____ before the Lord with all their might, with songs and lyres and _____ and tambourines and castanets and cymbals . . . and David _____ before the Lord with all his _____ . . . so David and all the house of Israel brought up the _____ of the _____ with shouting and with the _____ of the horn."

(2 Samuel 6:5—15)

II. Read the description in your book of how David and his men danced before the ark. Then, in the space below, draw a picture of what you imagine this scene looked like.

CHAPTER 14

King Solomon and
The Promise of a New King

I. Use your book to answer the following questions. The first letter of each word is given to help you. Write the number of letters in your answer in the right hand column across from the question. After completing the exercise, total the right hand column.

1. What did Solomon become famous for? w_____   _____

2. Solomon was the son of D_____.   _____

3. What did Solomon build? t_____.   _____

4. Where did he build it? J_____.   _____

5. Who predicted that the servant of God—the Messiah—would be

   beaten and killed for his people? I_____.   _____

6. Isaiah was a p_____.   _____

                                        TOTAL: _____

Your total should be 39 letters. If you did not get 39, maybe one of your answers is wrong or perhaps you misspelled a word. Go back and check your work.

II. Use your book to answer the following questions:

1. What did Solomon ask for when God asked him what he wanted? _____

_____

2. Why do you think that he asked for that? _____

_____

_____

3. What did God give him? _____

_____

_____

4. What would you ask for if God asked you what you wanted? _____

_____

_____

5. Why would you ask for that? _____

_____

_____

CHAPTER 15

The Final King

I. Circle the correct words hidden in the puzzle below to complete the sentences that follow. Use your book if you need help. *Hint*: Some answers may be longer than one word.

```
J  J  E  S  U  S  P  L  E  D
J  O  R  D  A  N  R  D  W  H
U  H  J  O  H  S  O  L  H  O
D  N  E  V  O  P  K  D  O  E
A  T  W  E  L  J  I  K  L  S
H  H  O  Y  P  S  I  I  Y  T
J  E  R  S  P  O  B  N  S  U
O  B  L  U  L  N  P  G  P  S
J  A  D  S  E  J  L  J  I  T
E  P  R  O  P  H  E  T  R  H
J  T  D  I  S  D  A  V  I  D
U  I  A  J  I  E  S  T  T  E
S  S  I  N  S  J  E  S  S  E
U  T  E  S  N  S  D  J  V  D
```

1. Who was baptizing outside of Jerusalem?
2. John was a great _____.
3. What was the name of the river where John was baptizing people?
4. John told the people to be sorry for their _____.
5. What special person did John baptize?
6. Jesus was a descendant of _____ from the tribe of _____.
7. When Jesus was baptized, the _____ _____ came down out of the Heavens in the form of a _____.
8. God the Father's voice was heard, "This is my beloved _____ in whom I am well _____."
9. Jesus was the last and greatest _____ of Israel.
10. But Jesus said, "My Kingdom is not of this _____."

31

II. Write "T" if a statement is true; write "F" if it is false. *Hint*: Use your book if you need help and read the statements *very* carefully!

_____ 1. King Nebuchadnezzar conquered Jerusalem and took the Hebrews to live in Babylon.

_____ 2. When the people of Israel were allowed to return to Jerusalem from Babylon, they rebuilt the Temple.

_____ 3. Joseph the Baptist lived in the desert, and he told people to be sorry for their sins because the new king was about to come.

_____ 4. Some people thought that John might be the king they were waiting for.

_____ 5. John said he was the new king when people asked him.

_____ 6. When Jesus was baptized the Holy Spirit came down in the form of an eagle.

_____ 7. Jesus was exactly the kind of king that everyone had been expecting.

CHAPTER 16

An Invitation to Heaven

I. God has given us an immortal soul, which is different from those of other animals. List three ways in which you can use your mind but in which a dog or cat cannot.

1. _____

2. _____

3. _____

II. Unscramble the words in parentheses to complete the sentences below. Use your book if you need help.

1. Jesus (senivit) _____ us to follow him and to come to Heaven.

2. Jesus does this because he (sevol) _____ us.

3. But Jesus will not (crofe) _____ us to say ''yes'' to his invitation.

4. God has given us a (refe liwl) _____ _____, which means that we have the power to say ''yes'' or ''no'' to Jesus' invitation.

5. But Jesus wants us to say ''yes'' very much. He even helps us to say ''yes'' by giving us his (crage) _____.

III. Use your book to answer these questions:

1. What are the ten ways that God gives us that help us say ''yes'' to his invitation to love him and others? _____

2. What did the Jews build to keep the Ten Commandments in? _____

_____

3. What do the first three Commandments help us to do? _____

_____

4. What do the last seven Commandments help us to do? _____

_____

CHAPTER 17

Road Signs Along the Way

Use your book (both Chapters 16 and 17) to answer the questions below and discover a message about the Ten Commandments.

☐ _ _ _ _ _ _

_ ☐ _ _ _ _ _ _ _

_ _ ☐ _

_ _ ☐ _

_ ☐ _ _ _ _ _

☐ _ _

☐ _ _ _

☐ _ _ _ _ _ _

☐ _ _

☐ _ _ _ _ _

☐ _ _ _ _ _ _ _

☐ _ _ _ _ _ _

_ _ _ ☐

_ ☐ _ _

☐ _ _ _

_ _ _ ☐ _

_ _ _ _ ☐

1. Always use God's name with _____.

2. Name of the place where Moses received the Ten Commandments.

3. We should _____ to God every day.

4. Keep the Lord's _____ holy.

5. On Sunday, we participate at _____.

6. In an oath, we use God as our _____.

7. The first three Commandments help us to love _____.

8. Do not take God's _____ in vain.

9. Name for Saturday, the Jewish rest day.

10. How many Commandments did God give Moses on Mt. Sinai?

11. The last seven Commandments help us to love _____.

12. Special days like Sundays.

13. The Commandments are all about _____.

14. Using God as your witness is called swearing an _____.

15. Do not take God's name in _____.

16. Who received the Commandments on Mt. Sinai?

17. We should listen to our religion teacher to _____ about God.

35

CHAPTER 18

Loving Others

I. Can you list three ways in which your parents have shown their love for you?

1. _____

2. _____

3. _____

II. The Fourth Commandment tells you to love, obey, and respect your parents. List at least one way in which you plan to show your parents tonight that you

1. Love them _____

   _____

2. Obey them _____

   _____

3. Respect them _____

   _____

Now, make sure that you do not forget to do these things tonight!

III. Write what you should do in each situation described below and then write which Commandment helped you to make your decision:

1. Your mother has told you to come right home after school, but since she will not be there tonight, she would not even know if you stopped at a friend's house for an hour before you went home. _____

   _____

2. In your class there is a person that everyone makes fun of and teases. _____

   _____

   _____

3. Sometimes your brother makes you so angry that you feel like hitting him. _____

   _____

   _____

4. Your mother asks you to help with the dishes even though it is not your turn to help.

   _____

   _____

5. Your babysitter tells you to go to bed, but you feel like staying up for a while longer.

   _____

   _____

6. Your friend is angry at you and does not want to be friends anymore. _____

   _____

   _____

7. Someone who has made you angry comes up to talk to you at school. You feel like
   ignoring him and walking away. _____

   _____

8. You are having your favorite dessert. You want to have a second helping but you
   know you will feel sick if you do have it. _____

   _____

9. You feel like teasing your little brother about his new haircut. _____

   _____

   _____

10. Someone you do not like is being punished. _____

   _____

CHAPTER 19

Growing in Love

The Father of Lies

I. If we follow the Eighth Commandment, we will love the truth. Solve the crossword puzzle below which lists some ways of not loving the truth.

Across

  1. False praise
  2. Untruths
  4. Worthless and useless talk about others.

Down

  3. Building up the truth to make it seem bigger or more exciting.
  5. Falsely _____ someone else for something you did.

Private Property

II. The Seventh and Tenth Commandments are about things that belong to others. Solve the crossword that tells us some things about private property.

Across

2. We must be careful with what others _____.
3. We must show _____ for other people's property.
5. The Tenth Commandment tells us that we should not even _____ other people's property.

Down

1. When we borrow something, we must be careful not to _____ it.
2. We must respect what belongs to _____.
4. The Seventh Commandment tells us: "You shall not _____."

III. Review the Sixth, Seventh, and Eighth Commandments.

1. Circle everything that the Sixth and Ninth Commandments tell us to do and cross out everything they tell us to avoid:

- Gossiping
- Disobeying your parents
- Stealing

- Pushing and shoving in line
- Filling your mind with what is good and pure
- Avoiding bad books, movies, jokes, TV shows

2. Circle everything that the Seventh and Tenth Commandments tell us to do and cross out everything they tell us to avoid.

- Gossiping
- Missing Mass on Sunday
- Being envious
- Learning about God
- Cheating on a test

- Wanting whatever someone else has
- Borrowing something and not returning it
- Praying
- Being patient
- Paying for something that we damaged

3. Circle everything that the Eighth Commandment tells us to do and cross out everything they tell us to avoid:

- Lying
- Telling a secret
- Gossiping
- Exaggerating

- Treating God's name with respect
- Flattering
- Sharing your candy
- Teasing someone

CHAPTER 20

Jesus, Our Guide

I. Write "T" if a statement is true; write "F" if it is false. *Hint*: Use your book and read the questions *very* carefully!

_____ 1. Jesus is half-man and half-God.

_____ 2. Jesus is one person with two natures.

_____ 3. Jesus is two persons with one nature.

_____ 4. Jesus is God.

_____ 5. Jesus is man.

_____ 6. How Jesus can be both God and man is a mystery.

_____ 7. How Jesus can be both God and man is easy to understand.

_____ 8. A miracle is something above the laws of nature and that only God can do.

_____ 9. Jesus worked miracles to show people that he is God.

_____ 10. Jesus is the only way to Heaven.

II. Unscramble the words to find what Jesus said to the Pharisees:

"FROEEB RHBAMAA ASW, I MA."

_____

_____

What did Jesus mean when he said these words? Use your book to help you answer this question.

_____

_____

_____

_____

CHAPTER 21

"For This I Have Come
Into the World"

Bible Arithmetic

I. Use your book to fill in the missing numbers in the following sentences.

1. Jesus was betrayed by __ of his __ __ Apostles.

2. Jesus said, "Destroy this temple and in __ days I will raise it up."

3. When Jesus said that he would raise up the temple, the Jews said that it had taken __ __ years to build.

4. Jesus remained on earth __ __ days after his Resurrection.

Add up all the numbers. You should come up with 102.

Mix and Match

II. Draw lines connecting the sentences beginning on the left with the proper endings on the right. Use your book if you need help.

Jesus' death . . .   . . . Jesus ascended into Heaven.

Jesus' becoming man . . .   . . . went to bring the souls of the good people who had died to Heaven.

After his death, Jesus . . .   . . . opened the gates of Heaven.

Forty days after he rose from the dead . . .   . . . is an honor to the human race.

III. Number the sentences in the order in which the events they describe happened.

_____ Jesus brings all the souls of the good people who have died to Heaven.

_____ Jesus spends time with his apostles and friends forty days before he ascends into Heaven.

_____ Jesus suffers and dies.

_____ Jesus rises on the third day after he dies.

_____ Jesus ascends into Heaven.

CHAPTER 22

The Perfect Sacrifice

I. Use your book to unscramble the words on the right in order to complete the sentences below:

1. The Mass is a _____. (FRASEICIC)

2. Jesus' Sacrifice of himself was and is _____. (TREEPFC)

3. The part of the Mass where we hear God's Word read is called _____ _____ ____ _____ _____. (ETH GRITYUL FO ETH DWRO)

4. The priest tries to help us understand God's Word in a _____. (LHIYMO)

5. The part of the Mass where Jesus becomes present on our altar is called _____ _____ ____ _____ _____. (HTE ITRGUYL FO HTE TRAHSICUE)

6. We must participate at Mass on Sundays and _____ _____ ____ _____. (YOHL YASD FO GLAITBIONO)

II. Write ''T'' if a statement is true; write ''F'' if it is false. *Hint*: Use your book and read the questions *very* carefully!

_____ 1. The Mass is the same Sacrifice as Jesus' Sacrifice of himself on Calvary.

_____ 2. The Mass is divided into three main parts.

_____ 3. The Liturgy of the Eucharist is the part where we listen as someone reads from the Bible.

_____ 4. The priest explains the Word of God to us in a homily.

_____ 5. The part of the Mass when the actual Sacrifice takes place and we receive Communion is called the Liturgy of the Word.

_____ 6. We must participate at Mass on Sundays and Holy Days of Obligation.

CHAPTER 23

Bread from Heaven

Mix and Match

I. Draw lines connecting the first part of each sentence with the correct ending.

You can eat
Living Bread . . .   . . . the bread becomes
                                            the true Body of Jesus.

When the priest says,   . . . every time you go
"This is my Body" . . .   to Communion.

Even the tiniest   . . . the wine becomes the
piece of the Host . . .   true Blood of Jesus.

Jesus is in the   . . . for you to come and
Eucharist . . .   visit him.

When the priest says,   . . . contains the whole Jesus:
"This is my Blood" . . .   Body, Blood, soul, and divinity.

Jesus waits in the   . . . because he wants you to
tabernacle . . .   receive him often.

II. What would you tell each of the boys and girls in the situations below? Use your book if you need help.

1. When Michael goes to Communion, the priest gives him a piece of a broken host.

   Michael is worried that he has not received the whole Jesus. _____

   _____

   _____

2. When it is time for Communion at Sunday Mass, Susan realizes that it has only been half an hour since she has eaten breakfast. _____

_____

What advice would you give Susan for the following Sunday? _____

_____

_____

3. Tom is trying to remember the three things he must keep in mind in order to receive Jesus worthily. _____

_____

4. Elizabeth wants to know at what point in the Mass the bread and wine become the Body and Blood of Jesus. _____

_____

5. Jim's Lutheran friend, Steve, is attending Mass with him. When it is time for Communion, Steve asks if he can receive Communion, too. _____

_____

_____

6. Sarah wonders when Jesus first gave us himself as Living Bread. _____

_____

_____

7. Robert wants to know what happens when Jesus comes to live inside us after we receive him in Communion. _____

_____

8. Ann wonders if there is any way to visit Jesus in the Blessed Sacrament when it is not time for Mass. _____

_____

CHAPTER 24

Mistakes Along the Way

I. Circle the correct answer to complete each sentence below. Use your book if you need help.

1. The judgment you make about how you ought to act or not act is called your

   a) context   b) conscience   c) constant

2. When we do something that we know is against God's laws, it is

   a) an accident   b) a temptation   c) a sin

3. The type of sin we can commit that kills all love for God is

   a) original sin   b) mortal sin   c) venial sin

4. The sin that offends God in a smaller way than mortal sin is

   a) original sin   b) mortal sin   c) venial sin

5. Thinking something unkind about another is an example of a sin of

   a) thought   b) word   c) action   d) omission

6. Not doing the dishes when we were told to is an example of a sin of

   a) thought   b) word   c) action   d) omission

7. Telling a lie is an example of a sin of

   a) thought   b) word   c) action   d) omission

8. Cheating on a test is an example of a sin of

   a) thought   b) word   c) action   d) omission

CHAPTER 25

Turning Back to God

Sacrament of Penance Sheets

Tear out these pages, staple them together, and save them until you go to Confession alone or with your class.

The Ten Commandments

1. *I am the Lord your God; you shall not have other gods besides me.*

   Have I thought of God and have I prayed to him each day? Have I tried to learn more about God by paying attention when someone teaches me about him? Have I been willing to share my things with others?

2. *You shall not take the name of the Lord your God in vain.*

   Have I only spoken of God with reverence?

3. *Remember to keep the Lord's Day holy.*

   Have I gone to Mass each Sunday and Holy Day of Obligation? Have I paid attention and responded to the prayers at Mass? Have I made Sunday a day of joy and rest for my family and myself?

4. *Honor your father and your mother.*

   Have I obeyed my parents and teachers quickly and cheerfully? Have I obeyed the rules of my home and school?

5. *You shall not kill.*

   Have I been kind to everyone or have I hit, kicked, or hurt others on purpose in any way? Have I been willing to play with everyone? Have I made fun of or said mean things to anyone? Have I taken care of my health by eating the right food, etc.?

6. *You shall not commit adultery.*

   and

9. *You shall not covet your neighbor's wife.*

   Have I looked at bad books, jokes, stories, or TV shows on purpose?

7. *You shall not steal.*

Have I cheated in class or in a game? Did I steal or keep things that are not mine? Did I take care of and return things that I borrowed?

8. *You shall not bear false witness against your neighbor.*

Have I told the truth? Did I say things about others that are not true? Have I flattered others for my own gain? Have I exaggerated? Have I gossiped?

10. *You shall not covet your neighbor's goods.*

Have I worried or complained that others might get or have more than I do?

Steps for a Good Confession

Check off each step as you complete it:

☐ 1. Examination of Conscience

Think about the Ten Commandments listed above and about whether you have broken any of them. Ask yourself the questions that follow each Commandment.

☐ 2. Tell Jesus you are sorry for the sins that you have committed. Ask for his help to make you truly sorry and for his grace so you will not commit those sins again.

☐ 3. Make up your mind that you will avoid those sins in the future.

☐ 4. Go into the confessional. Tell the priest your sins. Listen for any words of advice from the priest about how you can become better. Also, listen for your penance. Say an Act of Contrition:

O my God, I am heartily sorry for having offended thee. I detest all my sins because of thy just punishments, but most of all because they offend thee, my God, who art all good and deserving of all my love. I firmly resolve, with the help of thy grace, to confess my sins, to do penance, and to amend my life. *Amen.*

☐ 5. Do the penance the priest has assigned to you.

CHAPTER 26

The Holy Spirit

I. Write "T" if a statement is true; write "F" if it is false. *Hint*: Use your book and read the questions *very* carefully!

_____ 1. There are three Gods: the Father, the Son, and the Holy Spirit.

_____ 2. God the Son is Jesus.

_____ 3. The Holy Spirit is the Second Person of the Holy Trinity.

_____ 4. The Holy Spirit came down in the form of a dove at Jesus' baptism.

_____ 5. The Holy Spirit is the love between the Father and the Son.

_____ 6. We worship a different God than the one Abraham worshipped.

_____ 7. All three Persons of the Holy Trinity are one and the same God.

_____ 8. The first time the Holy Spirit came into your soul was at your Baptism.

_____ 9. Confirmation is the sacrament where the Holy Spirit comes and makes us even stronger followers of Jesus.

_____10. The Holy Spirit filled the apostles and the mother and friends of Jesus with his strength on Pentecost.

II. Reread the account in your book of the coming of the Holy Spirit at Pentecost. Then see if you can fill in the blanks in the Bible account below, using the following words: house, Holy Spirit, prayer, Heaven, fire, Jerusalem, Jesus, joy, Pentecost, wind, power.

"Then (Jesus) said to them . . . 'Stay in the city, until you are clothed with _____ from on high.' Then he led them out as far as Bethany, and lifting up his hands he blessed them. While he blessed them, he . . . was carried up into _____. And they worshipped him and returned to _____ with great _____ . . . ."

(Luke 24:44−53)

"Then they . . . went up to the upper room, where they were staying. . . . All (the apostles) devoted themselves to _____, together with the women and Mary the mother of _____. . . . When the day of _____ had come . . . , suddenly a sound came from Heaven like the rush of a mighty _____, and it filled all the _____ where they were sitting. And there appeared to them tongues as of _____, distributed and resting on each one of them. And they were all filled with the _____ _____. . . . ."

(Acts 1:12−Acts 2:4)

CHAPTER 27

The Church of Christ

I. Look up the definitions for the following words in Words to Know at the back of your textbook.

1. Mystical Body of Christ: _____

_____

_____

2. bishop: _____

_____

_____

3. Pope: _____

_____

_____

4. infallibility: _____

_____

_____

II. What would you tell each of the boys and girls in the situations below? Use your book if you need help.

1. Steve tells his Lutheran friend, Bill, that he is not Jesus' follower because he is not in the Catholic Church. _____

_____

_____

2. Katie says that it does not make any difference which church one belongs to. _____

_____

_____

_____

3. Tony says that unless the words of the Pope and the bishops are guarded by infallibility, we do not have to listen to them or obey them. _____

_____

_____

_____

4. Margaret says that we cannot be sure that we are receiving Christ's teaching two thousand years after he ascended into Heaven. _____

_____

_____

5. Greg would like to know who the first Pope was and who the Pope is now._____

_____

_____

6. Nancy says that it is not anyone else's business what she does. Her sins only hurt herself. _____

_____

_____

CHAPTER 28

Channels of Grace

I. Mix and Match:

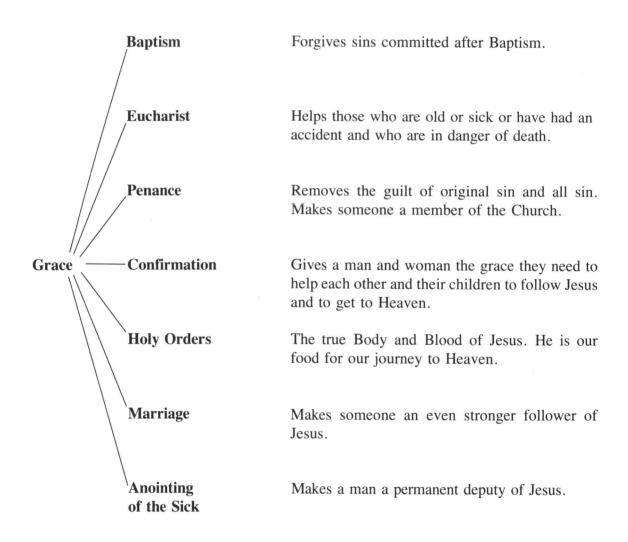

Baptism   Forgives sins committed after Baptism.

Eucharist   Helps those who are old or sick or have had an accident and who are in danger of death.

Penance   Removes the guilt of original sin and all sin. Makes someone a member of the Church.

Grace ——— Confirmation Gives a man and woman the grace they need to help each other and their children to follow Jesus and to get to Heaven.

Holy Orders The true Body and Blood of Jesus. He is our food for our journey to Heaven.

Marriage   Makes someone an even stronger follower of Jesus.

Anointing of the Sick Makes a man a permanent deputy of Jesus.

II. Here is the story of Joe, who received all seven of the sacraments. Use your book to help you fill in the name of each sacrament Joe received.

When Joe was a few weeks old, his parents took him to church and he became a member of God's family. Joe received the sacrament of _____. When Joe was in second grade, he and his class went to church where they confessed their sins for the first time. They received the sacrament of _____. In this way Jesus could help them to be better Christians. Later on in the spring of that year, Joe received Jesus under the appearances of bread and wine for the first time in his life! What a special day! He received the sacrament of the _____.

As Joe grew older, he continued to receive the sacraments of Penance and the Eucharist so that he would become more and more like Jesus. One day, when Joe was in eighth grade, Joe's teacher announced that the class was going to prepare to become even stronger followers of Jesus Christ. The day finally came when Joe and his classmates received the sacrament of _____.

Joe went to high school and college. After he graduated from college, he met a girl named Rose. He and Rose fell in love and were married. They received the sacrament of _____. Joe and Rose had a happy life together. They stayed close to God, and they taught their children about God and how to grow closer to him.

Later, when their children were grown, Rose became very sick and died. Joe was very sad because he missed her, but he trusted that she was with Jesus. After a few years, Joe felt a great desire to serve God by helping others to become holy. Since he was older and had been married, he needed special permission to study to be a priest. Finally, the wonderful day came when Joe was ordained to be Jesus' special representative. He received the sacrament of _____ _____.

Father Joe spent the remaining years of his life celebrating Mass and hearing confessions. One day the ambulance came and rushed him to the hospital. The priest at the hospital said some prayers over Father Joe and anointed his head and hands with oil.

Now Father Joe had received the sacrament of the _____

____ _____ _____. He died a few days later, but he was happy to go to be with Jesus

in Heaven.

CHAPTER 29

Our Mother, Mary

I. Use your book to solve the crossword puzzle.

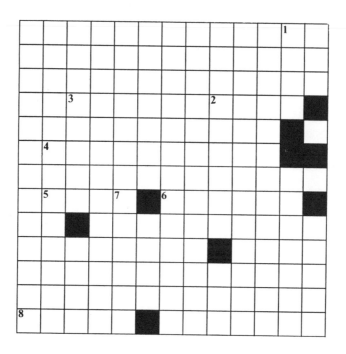

Across

2. The name of our Heavenly Mother.
4. The taking up of Mary's body and soul into Heaven.
5. When we pray to Mary, she _____ Jesus to help us.
6. Mary is watching over us from _____.
8. You are Mary's own _____.

Down

1. When we talk to Mary and ask for her prayers, we _____ to her.
2. Mary is our Heavenly _____.
3. Mary always leads us to _____.
7. Mary is sometimes called the _____ Eve.

II. Write your Mother in Heaven a letter. But first, take a minute to stop and think about Mary in Heaven and how she is watching you right now. She will really understand what you write to her. You can tell her or ask her whatever you want.

Dear Mother in Heaven,

_____

_____

_____

_____

_____

_____

_____

_____

_____

_____

_____

_____

Love,

_____

(Sign your name here.)

CHAPTER 30

We Reach Our Goal

I. Write a description of what you think it will be like to meet Jesus when you die.

_____

_____

_____

II. Draw lines to connect the words in the left column with the matching words in the right column.

General Judgment

Heaven

thoughts, words, actions, and omissions

end of the world

Particular Judgment

Hell

Purgatory

resurrection of the body

when Jesus will return to earth again

never-ending separation from God

suffering after death which purifies souls and helps them to make up for their sins committed while they were alive

the raising of all bodies from the dead and the reuniting of them with their souls at the end of the world

the judgment of the entire human race at the end of the world

eternal life and happiness with God

the things that Jesus will judge us on

the individual judgment of each person by Jesus

ADVENT AND CHRISTMAS SUPPLEMENT

I. During Advent, we often make a Jesse Tree to show some of the ancestors of Jesus and also those who prepared the way for his coming. Here is a list of some of those people.

Joseph—robe _____

Abraham—knife _____

Ruth—wheat _____

Isaac—wood _____

David—crown _____

Mary—lily _____

Adam and Eve—apple _____

Describe how each person helped to prepare for the coming of Jesus. Then draw and color a picture of the symbol listed by each name. Cut out your pictures, put hooks through them, and hang them on your Christmas tree or draw a big tree for them.

II. Ask your family or class if they will keep the custom of *Kristkindl* with you this year. *Kristkindl* is a German word which means "Christ Child". We prepare for the "coming" of the Christ Child by serving him in others. Here is how to do this.

1. The name of each person is written on a slip of paper and placed in a box. Then everyone draws a name. The person you draw will be your *Kristkindl*. He will represent the Christ Child for you in this time before Christmas. You will do things for him as if you were doing them for Jesus himself, but you must not let that person know who you are.

2. Each day of Advent, you do something special for your *Kristkindl*, without letting him find out that it is you who is doing it. It can be a sacrifice or a prayer, or it can be some special action to help him—but be careful not to get caught! While you are doing this for your *Kristkindl*, someone else is doing the same thing for you.

3. At Christmas, you prepare a small present for your *Kristkindl*. You also write him a note telling him who you are and some of the things that you have done for him.

60

LENT AND EASTER SUPPLEMENT

I. Check the things that you have done to prepare for Jesus' Resurrection at Easter.

☐ Went to Confession
☐ Gave some money for the poor
☐ Obeyed my parents cheerfully and promptly
☐ Offered up a little ache or pain to Jesus without complaining to anyone
☐ Did a kind deed for someone in my class
☐ Did a kind deed for my parents

☐ Participated at Mass and went to Communion on a weekday
☐ Did a kind deed for an elderly person
☐ Did a kind deed for a brother or sister
☐ Gave up something I like, like candy or a TV show
☐ Stopped in a church to visit Jesus in the Blessed Sacrament
☐ Said some extra prayers

II. Below are listed some symbols of Jesus' death and Resurrection. Find out what each symbol below stands for.

egg _____

_____

lamb _____

_____

lily _____

_____

butterfly _____

_____

purple and yellow _____

_____

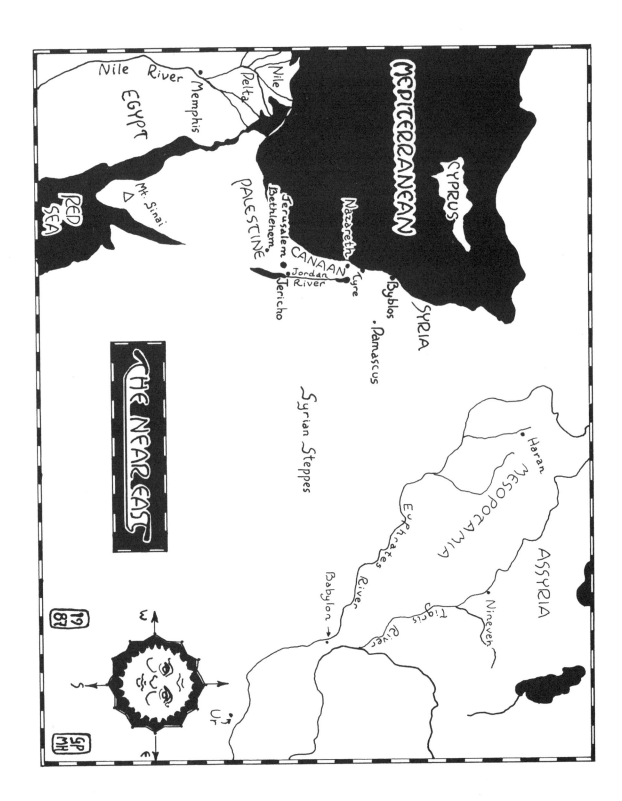

Map of the Holy Land

Here is a map of the ancient Near East. Follow the instructions below.

1. Put a **1** on the city where the Temple was.

   Who built the Temple? _____

2. Put a **2** on the city where King David was born.

   Do you know who else was born there? _____

3. Put a **3** on the land where the people of Israel were kept as slaves by Pharaoh.

4. Put a **4** on the river that the people of Israel crossed into the Promised Land. What else happened in this river? _____

   _____

5. Put a **5** on the Promised Land.

6. Put a **6** on the city where Abram was living when God first called him.

7. Put a **7** on the town where Jesus grew up.

8. Put an **8** on the sea that God parted to help the people of Israel escape from the Egyptians.

9. Put a **9** on the mountain where Moses received the Ten Commandments.

10. Put a **10** on the place where the people of Jerusalem were led into exile.

11. Put an **11** on the first city conquered by the children of Israel when they crossed into the Promised Land.